Bitcoin

The Impacts of Bitcoin, Special Guide and Tips for Beginners and Advances that Do Transactions and Invest in Bitcoin

Table of Contents

Introduction 1
Chapter 1: What is Bitcoin? 3
Chapter 2: Understanding the Blockchain and Transactions with Bitcoin 11
Chapter 3: How is Bitcoin Different Than Traditional Currencies? 14
Chapter 4: What Is Mining Bitcoin? 19
Chapter 5: Is Bitcoin Really That Secure? 27
Chapter 6: How Bitcoin is Changing Our Economy? 35
Chapter 7: The Benefits of Using Bitcoin 42
Chapter 8: How to Earn Money by Investing in Bitcoin 46
Conclusion 53

© Copyright 2017 by Noah Gladwyn - All rights reserved.

The follow eBook is reproduced below with the goal of providing information that is as accurate and reliable as possible. Regardless, purchasing this eBook can be seen as consent to the fact that both the publisher and the author of this book are in no way experts on the topics discussed within and that any recommendations or suggestions that are made herein are for entertainment purposes only. Professionals should be consulted as needed prior to undertaking any of the action endorsed herein.

This declaration is deemed fair and valid by both the American Bar Association and the Committee of Publishers Association and is legally binding through-out the United States.

Furthermore, the transmission, duplication or reproduction of any of the following work including specific information will be considered an illegal act irrespective of if it is done electronically or in print. This extends to creating a secondary or tertiary copy of the work or a recorded copy and is only allowed with an express written consent from the Publisher. All additional right reserved.

The information in the following pages is broadly considered to be a truthful and accurate account of facts and as such any inattention, use or misuse of the information in question by the reader will render any resulting actions solely under their purview. There are no scenarios in which the publisher or the original author of this work can be in any fashion deemed liable for any hardship or damages that may befall them after undertaking information described herein.

Additionally, the information in the following pages is intended only for informational purposes and should thus be thought of as universal. As befitting its nature, it is presented without assurance regarding its prolonged validity or interim quality. Trademarks that are mentioned are done without written consent and can in no way be considered an endorsement from the trademark holder.

Introduction

Congratulations on downloading this book and thank you for doing so.

The following chapters will discuss some of the different parts that come with working in Bitcoin. Cryptocurrencies have grown over the years, even though they are relatively new, and Bitcoin is one of the leaders of the pack. It is a great way to remain anonymous online, protecting your personal information while making it easier to shop and do other transactions at the same time. So many people enjoy working with cryptocurrencies that it is sure to make an even bigger impact on our financial future as the years go on.

This guidebook is going to take some more time to explore Bitcoin and all that you need to know about this particular cryptocurrency. Some of the things that we will discuss inside this guidebook include what Bitcoin is, how blockchain works to make the Bitcoin network successful, how Bitcoin can be so different from the traditional currencies we are used to, what mining Bitcoin is, and even how to invest in Bitcoin to earn money. There is just so much to learn and explore with this cryptocurrency, and you can even use it to make your own money in the process.

When you are ready to learn more about Bitcoin and how it works and move you up to a more advanced level, make sure to check out this guidebook and learn everything that you need to know about Bitcoin.

There are plenty of books on this subject on the market, thanks again for choosing this one! Every effort was made to ensure it is full of as much useful information as possible, please enjoy!

Chapter 1: What is Bitcoin?

The first thing that we need to talk about is the basics of Bitcoin and how it works. To keep things simple, Bitcoin is a digital currency that was created through the code and is held on the Bitcoin network. Unlike traditional currency, no one controls this currency, and there is no paper form of the currency. Bitcoin is produced by people, and even businesses are starting to use this, and the process of mining can help to create more Bitcoin for consumers to use.

Cryptocurrency has really been growing in the past few years. Many people are tired of using traditional currencies because they are worried about governments and banks having that much control. Bitcoin and the blockchain technology that goes behind it helps to make transactions faster and more efficient compared to traditional banking methods which have added to the popularity of this kind of currency. Add in that many people like Bitcoin because of the security that comes with it, and the anonymity, you will be able to make purchases and receive money without having to worry about other people getting ahold of their information.

How Is Bitcoin Different?

The first question that people will have when they hear about Bitcoin is how is it different from some of the other currencies, the traditional currencies, that we are used to seeing. Bitcoin is a currency that you can use online, which is similar to working with traditional currency, but it is only available and traded digitally.

Outside of being able to use it to make purchases and trade the Bitcoin online, there are many differences between this cryptocurrency and traditional currencies. To start, Bitcoin is not backed by a government agency or bank like the currencies that we are used to. This is good news for some people who are tired of seeing a separate entity decide inflation and other things about how much the currency is worth.

There also isn't any paper money to deal with. Everything is done online, from purchasing Bitcoin to making trades online and even investing and there really isn't any way to print off the money and use it that way. This is part of how the system works because the blockchain will keep track of all the transactions that happen in this system, keeping the information in order and keeping it all safe. While some people may not feel that comfortable working with a currency that they are not able to feel or see, it is kind of like working with a credit card, and you can always take the Bitcoin and convert it to whatever traditional currency you want as well.

Who Created It?

The idea behind Bitcoin was developed by the group called Satoshi Nakamoto. No one is sure about who is in this group, but he or she came up with the idea of Bitcoin as an electronic payment system that would be based on a mathematical proof. The whole idea of Bitcoin was for them to produce a currency that wasn't controlled by a central authority, one that could be transferred electronically, and one that didn't have many fees for the transactions.

One thing to realize is that you are not able to churn out as many Bitcoin as you want like a traditional currency. The code set it up so that there are only 21 million Bitcoins that miners can create. The good news is that these coins can be split up into smaller parts to help make it easier for people to use.

You may also be curious as to what the Bitcoin is based on to figure out its worth. The traditional currency has usually been based on either silver or gold. In theory (although this is not really something you can go and do), you could take a dollar to the bank and then get some gold back. Bitcoin is a bit different though. It is not based on gold or another precious metal because it is going to be based on mathematics.

Anyone who is using Bitcoin is using a software that follows a mathematical formula that produces the Bitcoin. This formula is available for anyone to use, so it is easy for others to check it out.

Characteristics of Bitcoin

There are a few features that are available with Bitcoin that help to make it a bit different than the traditional currencies that we are used to exchanging. Some of these characteristics include:

- Decentralized: The Bitcoin network is unique because it is not controlled by a central authority. Every machine that works with Bitcoin and mines this currency will make up the network, and they all work together. Many people like this idea because they can have freedom of using money without worrying how a central authority will try to manipulate it to meet their needs.

- Easy to set up: anyone who has spent time at a bank is used to having to jump through hoops to open up their bank account. And then if you want to have a merchant account, it can be even harder thanks to all of the bureaucracy that is involved. However, you can get started on the Bitcoin address in just a few seconds, and there aren't fees to deal with.

- Anonymous: There are a few steps that you need to take for this to happen, but it is possible to keep your identity hidden on the Bitcoin network. Your Bitcoin address is not going to show your personal address, name, or other information that would identify them.

- Transparent: the blockchain is set up to store all the transactions that occur on the Bitcoin network. If you have a Bitcoin address and have done any transactions on that network, the Blockchain is going to store that information.

- Smaller fees: compared to some of the fees that you may have to pay to your bank or other financial institution, the fees are very small on the Bitcoin network.

- Fast: it is possible to send money to anywhere in the world, and it will arrive in just a few minutes, much faster than some of the other options you are used to.

Bitcoin was one of the first types of cryptocurrencies available, and it has changed so much in the past few years. Many people are just starting to learn about cryptocurrency and how it can help them to make purchases all throughout the world, without having to give up their personal information or worry about how long the transaction will take. It is sure to make a big change in the way that we take care of finances in the future.

Remaining Anonymous

Many people like the idea that they are able to use the Bitcoin network in order to remain anonymous. They may be tired of using other online systems where their credit card and personal information can always be taken by anyone who wants to take a look at it. The fact that they can go on the Bitcoin network, do a few purchases, and have the information protected can be really appealing in today's world.

While Bitcoin is not completely anonymous, there are a few steps that users can take that will make it much harder for someone to look through and figure out which transactions are theirs. And for the most part, if you are good with your transactions (meaning not purchasing anything that is illegal or criminal in nature0, very few people are going to take a look at your information anyway, and you can stay safe.

Trouble with Criminal Activity

One of the biggest marks against Bitcoin and other currencies right now is the fact that there has been some criminal activity done on the network. Since the transactions are secure and mostly anonymous, it is easier for criminal activity to happen without being able to trace who did it. Whether items are being sold, money laundering, or even using Bitcoin as a way to avoid taxes, there is no doubt that some people throughout the world are using the network as a safer way to conduct their criminal activities.

While some people are exploiting the Bitcoin network, most users are staying safe and only using it for regular purchases and a more secure way to shop online. They like that the system remains anonymous, so they do not have to worry about others stealing their information or having to deal with identity theft. But because of the security that is found on Bitcoin, there are going to be some people who abuse the system.

How Governments Are Reacting

In reality, there have been a lot of different reactions to using Bitcoin depending on the country you are in. Some governments are all for these cryptocurrencies, choosing to embrace them and even design some of their own while others are working to close them down.

To start with is the United States. Lawmakers have been hard at work trying to shut down how this currency works. To start, they are making foreign policy that is requiring those in Russia and other governments to implement policies to stop transactions on Bitcoin that relate to terrorism. This can be hard to do with the anonymity that is present in Bitcoin and can really harm how well this currency is going to work. Also, the government is cracking down on the company Coinbase, claiming that they are going against IRS rules for not requiring participants to claim money for tax purposes. Coinbase is the primary exchange service in America for people who convert USD to Bitcoin or the other way around and if they option is taken away, it would be hard for Americans to use the network at all.

In China, there is a completely different approach. The Chinese government has decided to create their own cryptocurrency as a way to make it easier for all citizens to make payments and keep up with the economy, something that may have been difficult to do in the past in some parts. This is also a great way to strengthen the Chinese government and to make sure that their economy is going to keep on growing.

And of course, there is a wide range of reactions from governments throughout the world to the idea of cryptocurrency. Some are fond of the idea and are trying to find ways to make it more widely available and others are trying to stop it and stick with traditional forms of currency. No matter which method the government is taking, it seems like this cryptocurrency is gaining much traction and it is likely to stay around for a long time.

Chapter 2: Understanding the Blockchain and Transactions with Bitcoin

While Bitcoin has grown in popularity over the past few years and there are many people who have started to use Bitcoin, at least occasionally, for some of their purchases and to make money as well, the true wonder is the technology that makes all of this work. The blockchain technology makes all the difference, ensuring that all the transactions that occur on the Bitcoin network are recorded and stored on a ledger to keep it all in order. It does need the help of miners to keep this information safe, using special codes rather than just putting your information on the ledger, but all the transacttions will be available.

Let's take a look at how this blockchain works. When you first sign up for your Bitcoin address, you will get your own chain of the blockchain. As you start to make transactions along the way, this information is going to be added to the chain until it is filled up. Once the particular chain is filled up, it will join the permanent record and will be stored in the system. You will then receive a new chain that you can start filling up as well.

You can have as short of a chain or as long of a chain as you would like. The more transactions that you do, whether you receive money or you purchase something, you will see that this transaction is added to your chain. Those who go onto the Bitcoin network on occasion and barely do any transactions will not have a very long blockchain to work with. On the other hand, if the user spends much time on the network and goes through many transactions, they will have a longer blockchain.

As your blockchain starts to grow, it is going to join with the main blockchain for the whole network. It is like a bank ledger that anyone can see, but some safety precautions are placed on here to keep the information safe. Since anyone can look at the blockchain ledger, it would take them some work to figure out who is under each Bitcoin address, so your information is safe.

As the blockchain is designed, your information is going to be protected thanks to the miners. They are in charge of going through and providing a unique code to all the blockchain. Some specific rules come with the blockchain technology because it helps the information to stay safe and ensures that it does not become tampered with.

What this basically means (we will take a look at how the miners do their work later on), is that people can look at the ledger, but they will not see any of your personal information. This makes it much safer to use compared to using your credit card or another payment source with other forms of online shopping

The blockchain is actually the part of Bitcoin and other cryptocurrencies that are changing the world. The ledger system is fast and efficient, unlike the systems that are used by most banks and financial institutions in our modern times. Most of these companies are falling behind, wasting time, resources, and money, and the blockchain technology will help to make a big difference.

Without the help of blockchain technology, it would be really hard for Bitcoin and other cryptocurrencies to work properly. This technology is in charge of storing all the transactions and keeping them safe for anyone who takes a look through the ledger. It is also much faster and easier to use compared to some of the other options used in modern financial companies, making it something that many places could benefit from in the future.

Chapter 3: How is Bitcoin Different Than Traditional Currencies?

There are some similarities and some differences that come into play when we are talking about Bitcoin and comparing it to other currencies. For example, you are able to use Bitcoin in a similar manner to traditional currencies when you are shopping online. But the way that Bitcoin is formed is completely different compared to traditional currencies, and there isn't a central authority or government agency that is going to be in charge of the Bitcoin and will be able to mess around with it. This chapter is going to spend some time talking about how Bitcoin is different from other traditional currencies that we are used to.

The Value of Bitcoin

The first question that many people have about Bitcoin is what the value of it is. If they have one Bitcoin and they wanted to go onto the exchange to switch it out to US Dollars, how much would they expect to get back? At the time of this book, the current value of one Bitcoin is the equivalent of

$4,069.32 USD. Now, it is possible to break up the Bitcoin into some smaller bits so that you would end up with like $10 or another increment, and each of those has named as well so don't think you have to start out with over $4000 just to join the market

Since Bitcoin is shared all across the world and anyone who has a computer and signs up for the network can use this currency, there are conversion ratios for other forms of currency as well. For example, one Bitcoin will end up equaling 3,488 Euros.

The Similarities

Now let's take some time to see how Bitcoin is similar to the traditional currencies that we are used to. First, Bitcoin is used to make purchases or to receive money for a service or product that you provide. While most transactions are going to occur online through the Bitcoin network, there are an increasing number of traditional businesses who are joining this network so they can accept Bitcoin as a form of payment, just like they accept cash or credit cards.

Bitcoin is mostly saved for online shopping right now, with many companies going onto the network and accepting Bitcoin as one of their payment methods. Some brick and mortar stores do accept Bitcoin, as we discussed above, but they do have to have a special code reader, and it still goes through the network.

Bitcoin can also be exchanged for other currencies. We discussed this a bit in the last section, but it is possible to take your Bitcoin and change them out for Euros or US Dollars or another form of currency just like you can with traditional currencies. You can also use whatever traditional currency you currently have to purchase your own Bitcoin.

It is also possible to invest in Bitcoin-like you can with other forms of currency. Some even do forex trading with this, purchasing Bitcoin when the price is low and holding onto it when the real-world value is way higher. You can also invest in companies that are using Bitcoin, invest in the Blockchain technology, and so much more.

The Differences

There are actually quite a few differences that you will find when working with Bitcoin. The first one is that this currency doesn't have a central agency that is controlling it Most traditional currencies are run by the government or a bank, and sometimes it is a combination of these two. These entities are in control of the money, deciding how much the money is worth when to print more, and so on. Sometimes this can be effective at keeping inflation under control and provides some backing for the currency, but many people don't feel comfortable letting a big entity like the government get a say in how their money works.

Bitcoin does not have a central authority. While there was a central group that helped to create the whole Bitcoin network, they do not control how Bitcoin works after the code went live. They designed the code to do all the work, with a set amount of Bitcoin available from the start and no way to make more and kept all the authority figures out.

Bitcoin is also a currency that is done completely online. You are not able to order paper versions of Bitcoin, and if you want to use that money in a traditional store that doesn't accept Bitcoin, you will need to convert to your local currency. But there are many companies and individuals who accept Bitcoin, and you have many choices in the transactions that you use.

Bitcoin is considered a much safer currency to use compared to traditional currency as well. Since the blockchain is able to take care of the transactions and keep them secure, you won't have to worry as much about hacker or identity thieves getting hold of your information online. While there are some ways that a hacker is able to get this information if you make a lot of transactions online under the same address. But you can always change up your Bitcoin address and use other options to keep your information safe.

Another difference that you may notice is that the Bitcoin is not based off any precious metals. Most traditional currencies are based off silver and gold or the backing of the government, but this is not true when working with Bitcoin. Bitcoin was designed using mathematics and coding, which helps it to stay secure but doesn't give it a backing. The good news is that the code will help to determine how much the Bitcoin is worth and helps to make sure that you can use it no matter what.

There are some differences between Bitcoin and the other cryptocurrencies that you are dealing with, but often the differences are what makes Bitcoin so popular. They like that there isn't a government agency controlling the money and they like that it is controlled by mathematics rather than having to deal with inflation and other factors beyond their control.

Chapter 4: What Is Mining Bitcoin?

Now that we know a little bit more about Bitcoin, it is time to start talking about the process of mining. Mining is really hard to accomplish, and there are only a few people who can do it, but it is critical to the safety and security of all transactions on the Bitcoin network. Mining on Bitcoin is going to be the process of getting more Bitcoin by providing special codes that protect the transactions that occur on this network. There are people all over the world who work on this mining process so that they can earn more coins while helping out the network. Let's take a look at how this process works and why mining is so important to making sure that Bitcoin is successful.

How Does Mining Work

As we have mentioned a bit before, Bitcoin is growing quite a bit, and there are so many people from all parts of the world who have started to use this network to send Bitcoin to each other, make purchases, and sell products, with the amounts in each transaction varying based on what is going on. But without a good record of these transactions taking place, it could be hard to figure out if you made a payment or if the other person received their payment. This is why the Bitcoin network set up the blockchain to help them have a method of collecting and keeping track of all these transactions.

The miner is going to help make sure that these transactions are recorded on the Bitcoin ledger. They are in charge of confirming these transactions happened and then they will write it down on the ledger. There are a few rules that come into play before they can do the verification and ensure that the codes are done the right way before it is placed into the blockchain ledger.

So, the next question that you may have is what is the whole point of this ledger. We have talked a bit about blockchain and how it holds onto all the transactions that occur in the Bitcoin network, but why would we want to make sure that we wrote down this information and keeping track of it all the time? To keep things simple, this ledger is going to be a long list that will hold onto all the blocks that are created through the blockchain. You can take a look at this ledger to see what transactions have occurred on the network at any given time, which can be useful if you are keeping track of your own transactions or making sure that a payment went through for you.

Each user is going to receive a block that they can fill up with transactions as you use the system. Once the block is full, it is going to attach to the blockchain and will be stored permanently as part of the system. Of course, the more transactions that you do with this network, the longer this list is going to become because it shows everything that you ever do on this system. In addition, it can join the main blockchain in the network, and that list continues to grow over time as well. Anyone who is participating in the network will be able to get a copy o the blockchain so that they know what is going on with the system.

But, to have the system work, it needs to be trusted by the people who are using it. Since this is in a digital format, how is it possible for the users of this Bitcoin network to make sure that the blockchain stays intact and that someone is not able to come in and mess around with it? This is where the miners are going to come into the system and do their work.

Going back to the transactions, when one of the blocks on the blockchain is created and ready to be stored, the miners are going to get to work. They will take all the information that is found on the block, so all the transactions that the user did inside the block, and then add it to a formula that will turn it into something that is coherent but is something new. The result will end up being random, but something a lot shorter with a combination of letters and numbers called a hash. This hash is going to be placed inside the block, near the end of the blockchain that you just created.

Now, the hashes are going to seem a bit random, but there are a few properties and requirements that need to be in place, and this helps you to know if the hash is legitimate or not. It will be simple for the miners to take the data that your block created and create their hash, but since all of this is in numbers and letters, it becomes almost impossible to take a look at that data and figure out what it means. All hashes for all blocks in the blockchain need to be unique, and they will hold onto large amounts of data. These hashes will hide the information, but they also have to be unique to themselves, which is why if one does not match up, it will be instantly noticed. For example, if someone goes into the transactions and tries to make some changes, even to just one character, the hash will change and become something new.

Miners can use more than just the transactions to make the hashes that they need. They will sometimes use other information that is found inside the data as well. One important part that they will need to take a look at is the hash that is located on the block before this one on the blockchain.

Because all of the hashes in the block is going to be produced using the hash of whatever block was right before it, you are basically making it pretty secure, such as a wax seal in the digital world. This system is going to be able to confirm that this block, as well as the other blocks that follow it is legitimate because if someone comes in and tampers with it, everyone in the system would know.

This may all seem like much work, but the whole point is to help make sure that the system is going be secure. Because each hash in the block needs to use information from the block that came before it, you are adding in the equivalent of a wax seal to help keep the information safe. The Bitcoin system is going to have the opportunity to confirm that this block, and any blocks that come after it, are legitimate because if someone does come into the system and tampers with the information, everyone who is using the system would know about it. This helps to keep it all as safe as possible.

If you did go on the system and wanted to cause some trouble by faking a transaction, you would do so by going into one of the blocks that are inside the blockchain. However, once you change even one character, the hash for the whole block would end up changing. Another person would be able to go through these blocks, checking to see if they are authentic with the hashing function and they would quickly notice that one part was wrong. They would notice the changes that you made and now the one that is wrong and the one that is right, proving that there was a fake block pretty quickly.

Since all of the hashes are used to help create the next hash in line on the block, trying to tamper with the current block would mean that the block that follows it would end up with the wrong hash as well. This is a long-chain reaction that goes down through the code to the end, making everything end up out of line rather than matching up the way that they should.

While we did go through and add some depth to this process and how it can become more secure, the miners are basically going to be responsible for keeping track of the transactions that do occur inside of the Bitcoin system. They will use an approach that is randomized, and this helps to make sure that the system stays pretty secure, making it really hard for someone to just get into the system and mess around or write out false transactions.

The Competition for The Coins

Now that you have a little better idea of how the hashes work and how the miners work to keep the transactions safe, it is now time to learn how the miners are basically competing with each other to get more of these coins. The process is a competition and does take some work. Otherwise, everyone would decide to go with this process to make money. The miners will seal off a block with these hashes to keep everything secure, and when they are done, they will receive some Bitcoin. Once the miner can create one of these new hashes successfully, they will end up earning 25 Bitcoin, which is quite a bit of money.

This process ends up being a win-win for everyone who is involved. It helps the users of the network to keep their information safe and secure so that someone is not able to send out information that is false, so the system stays trustworthy. The miner can also do this so that they make money in the process. The money is a good incentive for the miner to keep up with the work because it can be hard and frustrating sometimes.

The biggest challenge that the miner will have when they are trying to create one of these hashes is that the Bitcoin network has made it a bit more difficult so that your computer is not able to just get the answers. It would be pretty easy to design a program to do this and then receive the Bitcoins that you wanted, but then everyone would do it, and the Bitcoin would all be mined at once.

The Bitcoin network has changed it up a bit and introduced a process that will check the proof of the work, which does make it much harder to create the hashes and get all the Bitcoin in no time. The protocol in Bitcoin will not just accept any hash that a miner gives to it because there is some protocol that has to be met ahead of time. First, the miner needs to make sure that the hash looks a specific way, with a specific number of zeroes occurring in the beginning. And when you use a computer or write out your hash, it is hard to have a good idea of what it will look like ahead of time until it is done. Anytime that someone adds some data to the system, it ends up changing the whole hash.

Working as a miner, it is important that when you are creating some of these hashes, you are not tempted to meddle with the data that is inside the transactions, but it is possible to move some of the data around in some cases to create a new hash. For example, the miner can bring in some other data, sometimes random, to help create a new hash. So, if you are working on some data that is just not working the way that it should for a hash, you could bring in some extra data, which is called a "nonce" to help change it up a bit.

As you can imagine, creating the hash can take some time, and it is not a process that you can work with overnight. Many miners will work on this full-time in the hopes of getting the Bitcoin and making some good money over a short amount of time, but you have to have a good amount of knowledge about computer programming and how this process will work.

Mining Bitcoins can be a good way for those who have a good grasp of computer programming to make some money. Since Bitcoin are currently worth so much in the market, the profit that you can make from working on a few hashes can make a big income. And it provides the users of the Bitcoin with the security they need to do transactions on this network without others figuring out who they are or taking their personal information.

Chapter 5: Is Bitcoin Really That Secure?

One of the reasons that many people choose to go with Bitcoin rather than sticking with traditional currency is because they believe that it has more security for the user. We live in a world where it is easier to make purchases online rather than running around town to find what we want. For those who want a specialty product, who need to run many errands in a short amount of time, or who do not live near any big stores that can help them, online shopping is often the best choice for them.

While it is common to do your shopping online, it can sometimes be dangerous. Some companies do not have the best security policies in place to help keep their consumer information safe, and even when you head to a regular brick and mortar business, there can be issues if you use your credit card. Hackers frequently try to get ahold of this information and use all the personal information that is accessible with your credit card. Credit card fraud and identity theft are on the rise and these numbers are expected to go up even more as people continue to shop online, and many companies are not able to keep up with the demand for the right kind of security.

Many people like the idea of using the Bitcoin network to keep their information safe. They like how the blockchain will hold onto all the transactions so they can look over them later on, but that the miners use their skills to help protect all the information inside. It is not possible for a hacker to get into the system and steal your credit card or other payment information. In some cases, such as using the same Bitcoin address many times over, hackers can still figure out who makes which purchases, but it is still much more secure compared to regular online shopping.

In addition to helping protect consumer and personal information, some people like to use the Bitcoin network because they want to make sure that no one can see what he or she are purchasing. In a world where it seems like all your personal information is readily available for others to use, it is nice when you can ensure that your information stays secure.

With that being said, Bitcoin is not completely safe and secure for you to use all the time. People can figure out who you are if you do not take the right precautions and if you make many different transactions under the same name and there is still some risk since it is all online. However, compared to some of the other online shopping methods, it is much safer. Let's take a look at some of the features that come with this network and why you will want to use it to stay safe and secure.

Why Do People Want to Stay Anonymous Online?

There are quite a few reasons why people will want to stay anonymous when they are online. The blockchain technology that comes with Bitcoin will help you to keep your personal information safe because others will not be able to figure out who you are. Many people like the idea of remaining anonymous including:

- Hiding transactions: Through the mining process we discussed before, the blockchain will make it easier for you to hide the transactions that you do online. If you would like an easy way to protect your information online, or you want to make sure that others are not able to see what you purchase, blockchain technology is the right option for you.

- Protect your information: Anytime that you are online looking around and making purchases, it is easy for others to follow you around. Whether you like to make purchases online or use social media, some of your personal information could be left behind. The blockchain technology can help protect your information because it will all be hidden inside the code, making it at least a bit harder for people to figure out which transactions are yours.

- Illegal activities: While the majority of the people who use the Bitcoin network will do so in a legitimate way to make money or to make purchases, there are some who will decide to work with cryptocurrencies because it helps them to perform illegal activities. This could be selling products that are illegal (either in their own country or the country they are selling to) or committing crimes like money laundering. Being anonymous helps these individuals get that work done.

- Security: The biggest reason that people will choose to go with the Bitcoin network and remain anonymous is that it helps them to stay safe online. Online transactions end up leaving a ton of information behind, and hackers love to look around and find this kind of information to use how they want. However, with the help of the blockchain technology found on the Bitcoin network, your information will stay safe and secure.

- Keep the government out of it all: There are many people who will choose to work with the various cryptocurrencies so that they make sure that the government stays out of the transactions they are doing. They may be tired of how the government and the big banks and other financial institutions can control the money and decide how much it is all worth. They will head online to keep their money safe and to make sure that no one can influence their wealth.

How Bitcoin Can Help You Stay Anonymous

Now, the Bitcoin network is not one hundred percent secure, which is true for any network that is online. Some hackers may have the time to get onto this network and learn who is making each transaction. The hackers will need to take some work to figure this out because linking the personal identity and address of the user together unless that user is really careless with how they behave online.

The good news is that there are a few little tricks that you can work on to make sure that your information will stay as safe as possible. According to the white paper that was released by the Satoshi company, it is recommended that users come up with a brand new Bitcoin address every time that they complete a new transaction on this network. This may seem like some extra work, but when you do this, it becomes pretty impossible to link your information back to you after the transactions are all done. Even if you don't change it after each transaction, doing it on occasion can help as well.

Another option is to work with a few different wallets as well. To keep things simple, the wallet is the place where you will complete all of your transactions and store the actual Bitcoin that you are using. If you use two or more wallets at the same time, it is much easier to keep your information safe and secure from other outside sources.

The good news is that there are a few different companies that create Bitcoin wallets that you can use and even some companies that help you to manage these wallets, so it does not become so hard. MultiBit is a good place to start because it works on all the operating systems, so you will not have to make any changes based on the computer you are working with. You can choose any of the companies that you like, but make sure that they are easy to use, secure, and will not lose your information.

One option that a lot of Bitcoin users like to stick with is a mixing service. With a mixing service, you will be able to take the Bitcoin that you earn and then trade them out to get the completely different history that is not linked to you. The mixing service is successful because it takes the coins from everyone who uses them, mixes them all around, and then gives some back to you that have a different history.

You will get the same amount of Bitcoins as you started with and basically, you will not see any difference in your account, but the Bitcoin will have different backgrounds and histories, so it is harder for people to put you with the transactions you have done on the network. In theory, this is very effective and helps you to stay anonymous on the network, but there are some places where there could be trouble. First, you have to trust the third part you are working with never to keep records of these transactions in the first place and you have to make sure that they provide you with the correct amount of Bitcoins back after switching them up. With a mixing company that is not reputable, you could end up losing all your Bitcoin.

E-wallets, or the parts that will hold onto your Bitcoin and keep track of your transactions, are another method you can use to help mask that you are the original owner of these coins. Some online wallet services will lump together the coins of all their users, much like the mixing services above, and then whenever you withdraw them, it will be with different coins than you started with. For this one to work, you need to make sure that the service you are using is already active and that other person is actively adding and withdrawing to the service as well.

The issue with these wallets is that they will keep track of all the transactions, or all the coins, that come with them and are taken out. You may end up with different coins than what you started with, but it can take away some of the anonymity that you were looking for. If you would like to remain anonymous with this option, you have to be careful with your transactions and make sure that they keep their records safe.

While the Bitcoin network may not be completely secure, there are some steps that you can take that will help you remain as anonymous as possible. You may have to put in a little bit of extra work to get it done, such as changing up your Bitcoin address each time you do a transaction or working with one of the mixing services to change the history of your coins, but for those who are looking to gain real anonymity, the work is not too bad.

Chapter 6: How Bitcoin is Changing Our Economy?

Bitcoin started out as a simple new currency that didn't have a central authority or government controlling it, and that could be used all over the world without having to worry about fees or other issues that traditional currencies do. But the neat technology that is on the Bitcoin network, the blockchain, really has the potential to make some big changes to our economy and people are starting to notice.

The first change is that many people are starting to prefer this currency over some of the traditional currencies that have been around for a long time. Bitcoin and other cryptocurrencies are growing in popularity and more and more people like that they are easy to use, their value isn't tied to a government, and that they can remain hidden while using the network.

There are already plenty of companies that use the Bitcoin network. Some are exclusively found on this network and will only sell products in this manner, but some other companies are starting to accept Bitcoin as a payment method, even sometimes indirectly. For example, you cannot use Bitcoin to make purchases directly with Amazon, but you can use Bitcoin to purchase Amazon gift cards and then shop with those.

As Bitcoin and the blockchain technology continue to grow, it is likely that there will be even more e-commerce that occurs with this currency. The money is available here right now, and many companies are going to be open to accepting it as a way to attract new customers to themselves in the future.

But this is not the only way that our economy is going to change in the future and most of the changes are going to occur thanks to the blockchain technology. In fact, several companies are already using this because it is so fast and effective compared to the other methods that are used.

When we do a traditional transaction, it often takes some time. We have to send the information over to the seller or the company, and they have to use this to contact the bank or the credit card company to get the money. The bank then has to verify all the information before sending the money over to the seller, and you can get your product. This process takes a long time because there is a middleman who is messing around and taking their percentage of the fees and so on in the process.

This process is not very efficient. No one likes waiting around for a product because the bank is taking too long with it. And the ledger system that is used by most banks and financial institutions is slow and won't get the job done in the timely manner that is should. Add to this that most of these institutions are losing millions of dollars each year to accounting errors and trying to maintain these ledgers, and you can see how this whole thing is pretty inefficient and outdated.

We are living in a world where we expect things to be instant. We are used to purchasing in just a few seconds, and it can be frustrating when it takes hours, and sometimes even a few days before the bank will even recognize the transaction. Why is it that our banking system is so far behind the technology that is present today? Blockchain technology can solve some of these issues by replacing the ledger system that is present at most banks and other financial institutions.

The blockchain technology uses a different kind of ledger system than what is found in the traditional banks. This system already has all of your information stored and ready, and it can use this to come together with the seller, so your transactions are instant. You will be able to pay the seller right away, without them having to wait forever to hear back from the bank, and your product will be on its way quicker than ever before.

Because the blockchain technology is more efficient and faster than traditional ledgers, there are already many companies who are considering using this technology to help them assist their customers better and to save themselves money. This alone will make a big difference in the economy, taking out some of the issues with the middle man and making it easier to complete the transactions that you want.

Other Ways Bitcoin Will Change the Economy

We have spent some time talking about Bitcoin and how it can change the economy. From getting more businesses to join this platform and use this kind of currency to making the blockchain technology more available on the market, this technology is making strides to change the way that we do business in the future. But we have only talked about a few of the ways that Bitcoin is going to change the economy in the future. Some of these include:

Money Transfers Across Borders

One reason that people like to use blockchain and Bitcoin is that they can use it to make international transfers of money. This could just be when you want to send money to a loved one who is living in another country or even when you are making a purchase online from someone who is located in another part of the world. In the past, it would take much work to transfer all of this money over to the right party. Often you would have to work through the governments of both companies and a converting party, who would charge much money in fees to make this happen.

Now it is much easier to use this technology to send money to other countries. You can make purchases or just send the money over when you need. The money will be available almost instantly to the other party, and the fees are pretty much non-existent at this part.

Since individuals can use this network to send money overseas, it makes sense that banks and other companies would be able to use this blockchain technology to send money as well. This could save hundreds of thousands in fees and other costs each year and will really make a big difference in how our economy works.

Securities Settlement and Clearing

Another area that is highly talked about regarding blockchain is the settlements. When you build settlement and clearing systems with the help of the blockchain, it can help to really reduce the costs that the companies are spending, but it can help to improve any inefficiencies that occur in the market by leveraging the technology.

There are a few different stock exchanges, including the Hong Kong Stock Exchange, the Australian Stock Exchange, and the Nasdaq are working with some blockchain based securities settlement systems because they think that it will reduce some of the costs while increasing the speed of the trades. There are other companies as well that are talking about creating these kinds of platforms with the help of the distributed ledger technology found in blockchain later this year as well.

Trade Finance

The blockchain technology is well known for being able to record, store, and transfer data securely, which makes it really great to apply to the supply chain and the finance sector. There are a few major banks in Europe announced that they are going to work together to build a blockchain platform to help with trade finance and supply chain management for small and medium enterprises in Europe.

The point of this is that the stakeholders will be able to securely track the transaction, from the first part of the trade all the way through. This is going to make it transparent, either with a web-based or mobile application. The point of working on this is to make it easier for cross-border transactions in Europe. This is something that could be used all throughout the world, helping to increase trade and keep the whole thing transparent at the same time.

Insurance

Another area that could benefit in the future from the use of blockchain is the insurance industry. There are a few startups that are working to change up this sector with the help of blockchain technology as well as with peer-to-peer models and artificial intelligence. One place that the insurance sector is going to do well with it with smart contracts. It would be pretty easy for an insurance policy to be created as a smart contract, meaning that the policy can be signed by both parties and then it will automatically pay out once some conditions are met. Many customers and clients would feel so much better-having control over the contract of their insurance policy without having to worry so much about calling the company and waiting for a response.

As you can see, it is possible for a lot of different things to change in the near future regarding how blockchain can help. Whether it is with smart contracts, with helping to make trades easier than ever before, or something else, blockchain is here to stay and will make a huge difference in how we conduct business in the future.

Chapter 7: The Benefits of Using Bitcoin

We have spent much time talking about Bitcoin and some of the ways that you can use this to get the full benefits of working online with your currency rather than working through traditional money. But you may still be curious as to why Bitcoin is so much better than some of the traditional forms of currency that you have used in the past. This chapter is going to talk about why Bitcoin is one of the best currency options to work with rather than sticking with the traditional currency.

The first benefit of working with Bitcoin, as well as many of the other cryptocurrencies that are available, is that the user can stay anonymous. When you do online shopping with other companies, it is really hard to remain private. Yes, your information is supposed to stay secure on the servers with the company, but it does not take that much effort for a hacker to get into this and steal the information that they want. Most people are tired of using credit cards, even at physical stores, because it seems like there is a breach almost every week.

But with Bitcoin, things are going to be a little bit different. The purchases that are on Bitcoin are going to be really discrete, and unless the user is going out there and publishing these transactions, they will have the benefit of their purchases not being associated with their identity. It is kind of like making purchases with only cash, almost impossible to trace.

Now, there are a few things that you will have to do in order to make sure you remain anonymous, especially if you complete a lot of transactions inside the Bitcoin network. You may want to use different Bitcoin addresses for the various purchases, so it is much harder to trace purchases back to you.

Another benefit that you will enjoy when you are working with Bitcoin is that there will never be any interruptions from third-parties who are trying to get ahold of the information. This is actually one of the most widely publicized benefits of the network and one of the reasons that many people like to stick with Bitcoin rather than just doing regular online shopping. Governments, financial intermediaries, and banks are not going to be able to get onto the system and interrupt any of the transactions or even put a freeze on the account of the Bitcoin user.

This is because the whole idea of the Bitcoin network is a peer-to-peer experience. Users will be able to enjoy quite a bit of freedom when they use the Bitcoin network compared to using traditional currencies because they will not have to worry about banks or other agencies getting into their business.

You may also notice that some of the purchases that you make with Bitcoin are going to cost a little bit less than they would through other mediums. This is because the purchases that you work with are not going to be taxed. Since you are not worrying about third parties identifying, tracking, and intercepting your transactions (as long as they remain in Bitcoin), you will not have to worry about any sales taxes being added to your online purchases.

You do need to be careful with this a little bit though, especially if you are earning money on the Bitcoin network. The United States government is trying to crackdown on those who earn money through means like Bitcoin and other cryptocurrencies who do not pay their taxes. Many people use the system and the fact that they can remain anonymous as a way to avoid their taxes. It is much better to always claim the money that you earn on Bitcoin to avoid any troubles if the government does find out.

Unlike some of the other financial institutions that you may have worked in the past, working on Bitcoin means that you get very low transaction fees. Anytime that you usually do a foreign purchase or a standard wire procedure, you are going to have a lot of exchange costs and fees. However, Bitcoin is different since there aren't any governments or intermediary institutions present, which means that the costs of these transactions are going to be low. As a traveler or someone who is trying to make an online purchase, this can be a big relief in the form of the fees that you pay.

Chapter 8: How to Earn Money by Investing in Bitcoin

While some people are happy just getting to use Bitcoin to remain anonymous in the purchases they are completing, there are some that see many opportunities when they look at the whole idea behind cryptocurrency. For those who want to make much money off this new currency, there are quite a few methods that you can try out. From investing right with the Bitcoin company to writing out smart contracts and so much more, you are sure to find a method that will work just right for you.

Invest in The Bitcoin Company

The first place you should consider investing with Bitcoin is in the company itself. Just like with other companies around the world, it is possible to purchase shares of the Bitcoin company and then earn dividends each quarter or sell them when the price goes up. Right now Bitcoin shares are very popular, and they are rising in price, so this is a great way for you to earn some extra money.

You do need to take precautions when you are going with this method. Just like with any company, you need to do your research about the market and have a strategy in place. This can outline how many shares you will purchase when you enter the market when you exit the market, and so much more. Having a sound strategy, even in a market that seems to be doing as well as Bitcoin, will help you to make as much money as possible.

Invest in The Blockchain Technology

The Blockchain technology is the backbone of how all of Bitcoin is going to work. And there are so many applications for this technology that is outside the world of Bitcoin and cryptocurrency as well. We talked about a few of the industries who could really see a difference if they started implementing blockchain including banks, financial firms, and even insurance firms. It is fast, efficient, secure, and everything that our modern world needs to help transactions get done.

If you are really looking for a way to make money off part of Bitcoin, investing in updates with the blockchain technology or in a company who is trying to develop a platform with this technology is a great place to start. Often these platforms can be used with more than one type of company, making it possible to see a large profit once the product is developed. And as we go into the future, there will be more applications of the blockchain discovered, making it possible for your investment to go even further

Find A Company That Works Through Bitcoin

There are many different ways that you can invest in this whole market, and one way is to invest in a company that is willing to use the Bitcoin technology. The companies who use Bitcoin or accept it as payment are the ones who are sure to see much growth shortly Working with them and investing in those, especially the ones that are just starting out and choosing to work with just Bitcoin, can help you to make much money.

Run Your Own Business

Some people decide to go a more traditional route to invest their money. If you have a business or plan on starting a new business, you may be able to profit by accepting Bitcoin as one of your forms of payment. Some people choose to use this as their only form of payment and will only work with customers on the Bitcoin network, while others will accept that and other forms of payment to reach customers who may not be on the Bitcoin network yet.

This is going to carry some of the same risks that you would see with a traditional business, whether you are working completely on the Bitcoin network or not. But since you are already providing services to a niche market, you are going to find a lot of potential customers who are ready to purchase things from you. If your business is already up and running, you may find on that adding the Bitcoin payment option will make you very popular on this network right from the beginning.

Forex Trading with Bitcoin

When we are working with the stock market, forex trading is basically trading in money. This is something that you could do with Bitcoin as well. You need to make sure that you understand the market as well, but it is a great way to earn money right now since the value of Bitcoin just keeps rising. In fact, Bitcoin is currently worth over $4000; just a few months ago it was worth closer to $2500. This is a huge increase.

To make this work, you would wait until the price of Bitcoin is down a bit, which means you need to get in on this as early as possible. Let's say that you bought in when the price of Bitcoin was just $2500 USD. You would have bought as many Bitcoin as you wanted or could at that price, and the just left the money there, watching to see what the market would do.

If you took the Bitcoin out now, you would have a profit of over $1500 per Bitcoin that you purchased. That is a huge amount of profit for such a little amount of time. You could hold onto the Bitcoin for a little bit longer and see if the market takes it up even more. This requires very little work from you and can yield much profit, especially since it is estimated that the value of Bitcoin will continue to go up for some time

You do need to have some patience when you work with this method though. If you look at the history of how much Bitcoin is worth, you will see that there are some fluctuations up and down, even though Bitcoin is so popular. This means that while the market may go down for a few months here and there, it will go back up as well. The dips are pretty limited, and the increases are pretty large so learning how to be patient is important. Some people get into Bitcoin and then see that the market goes down right away, so they panic and sell their shares. Those who have patience and wait out the market will see a great return in the process.

Create Smart Contracts

If you have a little bit of computer programming background, you may want to consider creating a smart contract. These can be used by many individuals and businesses in Bitcoin, and you can earn a small commission each time that one of your contacts is used.

A smart contract is going to be a series of computer protocols that are used to facilitate, verify, and even enforce a contract that the two parties agree on. These contracts will do the work on their own, executing as soon as the right conditions have been met by both parties. For example, a landlord and a tenant could use a smart contract to get set up. The tenant could give a small deposit to hold the location for a short amount of time. If the landlord gives the tenant the key by the specified date, the money will be released to the landlord, but if the key is not released, the money will go back to the tenant. This is a good way to protect both parties in the contract.

There are a lot of different ways that these smart contracts can be used and many companies could enjoy them. If a company has used a contract for another purpose in the past, they could use these smart contracts. The smart contract will do all the work while eliminating the need for a middleman in the process.

Now, there are many companies that need these kinds of contracts, and if you are able to create one, you could make some good money. You would just need to have the right code and a good template and let the other parties fill in the information that regards to them. Then you can charge a small fee, which is usually a lot less than they would pay with an intermediary in the process, to execute the code. This helps you to make money each time a contract is done on the network while helping other companies as well.

Invest in Individuals

Another method that you can use to make money when working with Bitcoin is to look for an individual who would like to start their own company or who has a great idea and invest in them. One of the cool things about Bitcoin is that it works off what are known as smart contracts. These are self-executing contracts that will execute as soon as certain conditions are met, without needing to use a bank or someone else in the middle to make it happen.

There are often going to be different individuals who want some capital to help them get started in their new industry, and they could design a smart contract to help get this done. You can come up with an agreement about how much you will give them, how long the terms are or, and how they will pay you back. This could be a good way to make money if you are just starting out and even better if you work with a few people who will put in money together.

As you can see, there are many different options you can use to help you earn money by investing in Bitcoin. This is a newer source of currency so there are bound to be a lot of startups and other options that you can choose that will help you earn much money in no time. Consider a few of these options, and you are sure to start making money in no time.

Conclusion

Thank for making it through to the end of this book, let's hope it was informative and able to provide you with all of the tools you need to achieve your goals whatever they may be.

The next step is to start working with Bitcoin with the method that is right for you. Many people are interested in getting into Bitcoin either to make purchases or to make money. Either way, the system is safe and secure to use, helping to get the transactions done quickly with all your information safe and sound. This guidebook has spent some time talking about Bitcoin and all the parts that you need to get the most out of this great cryptocurrency.

There is so much to learn about this new cryptocurrency, and many people are finding that it is the right choice for them to make secure purchases or even to make money. This chapter will go through some of the basics of cryptocurrency, such as how to get started, how the blockchain technology works, and even how Bitcoin is going to change the way we do business and our economy in the future. We will even spend some time talking about how you can use Bitcoin to invest your money and make a good income at the same time.

When you are ready to learn more about Bitcoin and how it works, and how you can put your money to work by investing in Bitcoin, make sure to take the time to read through this guidebook and learn as much as possible now!

Finally, if you found this book useful in any way, a review on Amazon is always appreciated!

www.ingramcontent.com/pod-product-compliance
Lightning Source LLC
Chambersburg PA
CBHW050022230526
45470CB00003B/1080